OSLO AND

BERGEN

TRAVEL GUIDE

AMARA CARMICHAEL

About the Author

Amara Carmichael an ardent traveller and seasoned writer with a passion for seeing other cultures and discovering fascinating locations. With years of expertise in travel journalism, I've written several travel periodicals, online publications, and guidebooks, sharing my experiences and suggestions with other travellers worldwide.

My numerous adventures have brought me across continents, allowing me to immerse myself in the local cultures, cuisines, and experiences that each place has to offer. My skill lies in producing informative travel guides, delivering important suggestions, and unearthing hidden treasures in renowned cities and off-the-beaten-path locales equally.

Through my engaging writing style and my experiences, I strive to inspire wanderlust and motivate visitors to go on unforgettable travels while navigating unfamiliar locations with confidence.

I am committed to sharing my enthusiasm for travel, delivering practical guidance, and assisting readers to make the most out of their adventures, guaranteeing amazing experiences wherever their wanderlust takes them.

TABLE OF CONTENTS

INTRODUCTION

Welcome to Oslo and Bergen

Welcome to the captivating cities of Oslo and Bergen, nestled amid Norway's breathtaking landscapes. This guidebook invites you to explore the unique blend of history, culture, and natural beauty that these cities offer. Whether you're drawn to Oslo's cosmopolitan charm or Bergen's old-world allure, this guide aims to be your companion, providing insights and recommendations for an enriching journey through these Norwegian gems.

Join me as we delve into the rich history, vibrant cultural scene, and stunning fjord landscapes, discovering the wonders that Oslo and Bergen have in store for you.

How to Use This Guide

This travel book is meant to be your thorough companion throughout your tour of Oslo and Bergen. Here's how you can make the most of it:

1. Navigation: Navigate through the table of contents to uncover particular parts relevant to your interests or vacation plans.

2. Destination Insights: Each part includes thorough insights into the attractions, neighbourhoods, restaurants, cultural

activities, and practical advice for both Oslo and Bergen.

3. Planning Assistance: Utilise the planning sections for ideas on ideal times to travel, transportation alternatives, entrance procedures, and visa information.

4. Neighborhood Guides: Explore local neighbourhood guides for each city to explore their particular charm, monuments, and things to do.

5. Practical guidelines: Refer to the practical information area for hotel possibilities, eating suggestions, safety guidelines, and relevant local terms to enhance your trip experience.

6. Appendices: Check the appendices for additional materials, maps, and an index to assist quick reference and exploration.

Use this book as your roadmap to experience the beauty, history, and cultural diversity of Oslo and Bergen, adapting your tour to meet your interests and tastes. Enjoy

your adventure!

Essential Travel Tips

For a seamless and pleasurable trip seeing

Oslo and Bergen, consider these key travel

tips:

1. Weather Preparedness: Norway's weather

may be changeable. Pack layers and

weather-appropriate attire, especially if you

plan to come during colder months. Always

have a waterproof jacket or umbrella.

2. Currency and Payments: Norway largely utilises the Norwegian Krone (NOK). Credit and debit cards are generally accepted, however it's essential to carry extra cash, especially for smaller places or in isolated locations.

3. Public Transportation: Both cities feature excellent public transit networks, including buses, trams, and ferries. Consider purchasing city travel cards or passes for convenience and savings.

4. Respect Local Customs: Norwegians emphasise timeliness and humility. When meeting locals, a handshake is traditional, yet keeping a polite distance during chats is preferred.

5. Tipping Culture: Tipping is not necessary in Norway as service costs are frequently included in invoices. However, rounding up the amount or giving a little tip for great service is appreciated.

6. Safety and Health: Norway maintains strict safety requirements. It's typically safe

to travel, but normal measures like securing things and being attentive of surroundings should be taken. Ensure you have travel insurance and are aware of emergency numbers.

7. Language: While most Norwegians speak English effectively, acquiring a few basic Norwegian words may enrich conversations and demonstrate appreciation for the local culture.

8. Exploring Nature: If planning outdoor activities or treks, be well-prepared with

suitable gear, maps, and knowledge of the region. Respect nature by adhering to 'leave no trace' ideals.

9. reserving in Advance: For popular sites, tours, or lodgings, consider reserving in advance, especially during high tourist seasons, to assure availability.

10. Adapt to Local Time: Norway observes Central European Time (CET). Adjusting to local time upon arrival might help overcome jet lag and make the most of your visit in these gorgeous towns.

By considering these vital guidelines, you may enrich your vacation experience and immerse yourself more thoroughly in the culture and beauty of Oslo and Bergen.

CHAPTER 1

BEGINNING YOUR

JOURNEY

Planning Your Trip to Norway

Planning a trip to Norway, especially to explore Oslo and Bergen, involves several key considerations to ensure a rewarding and seamless travel experience. Here's a complete resource to aid you in arranging your journey:

Best Times to Visit

Norway's climate varies throughout regions and seasons, influencing the ideal times to visit Oslo and Bergen. Summers (June to August) offer pleasant weather with extended daylight hours, great for outdoor activities and visiting the fjords. However, this period tends to be the peak tourist season. For fewer visitors and probable northern light sightings, try visiting in late autumn or winter.

Climate Considerations

Norway experiences diverse weather patterns. Oslo experiences somewhat milder temperatures, but Bergen tends to be rainier due to its seaside position. Be prepared for changing weather conditions by carrying suitable clothing and supplies, especially if planned outdoor excursions or treks.

Major Events and Festivals

Check the local event calendars for festivals, cultural events, or celebrations that could connect with your travel dates. From music festivals to traditional folk gatherings, experiencing experiencing these cultural celebrations can offer a distinct depth to your journey.

Seasonal Attractions

Each season in Norway unveils different attractions and activities. Winter offers options for skiing, snowboarding, and experiencing the magnificent Northern Lights. Spring offers blossoming landscapes and pleasant temperatures, great for trekking. Summer provides access to outdoor activities and a bustling city life.

Crafting Your Itinerary

Craft a flexible itinerary based on your interests and the duration of your visit. Allocate time for discovering historical monuments, enjoying outdoor activities, delighting in local food, and immersing yourself in cultural experiences specific to Oslo and Bergen.

Accommodation and Reservations

Book lodgings in advance, especially during peak tourist seasons, to secure your preferred choices. Consider the location, facilities, and closeness to attractions while picking hotels, hosts, or vacation rentals in both cities.

Budgeting and Costs

Norway is noted for its higher cost of living. Plan your budget appropriately, considering expenditures for lodging, food, transportation, and activities. Consider acquiring city passes or discount cards for attractions to save money.

Travel Documents and Insurance

Ensure you have a valid passport with ample validity, and if required, apply for the necessary visas well in advance. Additionally, consider travel insurance to cover against unforeseen occurrences during your vacation.

By meticulously planning and considering these aspects, you may adapt your journey to fit your preferences, ensuring a well-organized and memorable exploration of Oslo and Bergen.

Best Times to Visit

Determining the ideal time to explore Oslo and Bergen depends on several aspects, including weather preferences, desire activities, and the types of experience you seek. Here's a breakdown of the best times to visit these enthralling Norwegian cities:

Summer (June to August)

Oslo

- Summer in Oslo provides moderate temperatures, averaging approximately 15-25°C (59-77°F).

- Long daylight hours offer ample time for exploring outdoor sights like Vigeland Park, the Oslo Fjord, and the city's museums. - This period features numerous cultural events, concerts, and festivals, creating a dynamic atmosphere.

Bergen

- Summers in Bergen are milder but rainier, with temperatures ranging from 13-18°C (55-64°F).
- Despite occasional showers, this time offers beautiful green landscapes and

is perfect for exploring Bryggen, the fjords, and nearby hiking paths.

Autumn (September to November)

Oslo & Bergen

- Autumn showcases Norway's breathtaking fall foliage, painting the landscapes with bright colours.

- Temperatures start to dip, averaging between 5-15°C (41-59°F), but the crisp air and fewer crowds make it an excellent time for sightseeing and trekking.

Winter (December to February)

Oslo & Bergen

- Winter in Norway delivers a magnificent experience, especially for snow enthusiasts.

- Oslo offers winter sports activities in nearby areas and a chance to witness the Northern Lights in the northern regions.

- Bergen experiences mild winters, with temperatures about 0-6°C (32-43°F), creating a warm ambiance and a chance to explore Christmas markets and cultural events.

Spring (March to May)

Oslo & Bergen

- Spring brings flowering flowers and a sense of renewal to both cities.

- Temperatures steadily rise, ranging from 5-15°C (41-59°F), making it an ideal time for trekking, exploring parks, and enjoying outdoor activities.

Considerations:

- Peak Tourist Seasons: Summer months witness higher tourist numbers, leading to crowded sights and higher accommodation prices. Winter, on the other hand, might be crowded in famous ski resorts.

- Northern Lights: For a chance to witness the mesmerizing Northern Lights, plan a visit between late fall and early spring, particularly in northern regions.

- Outdoor Activities: Summer and early autumn offer the best conditions for outdoor adventures, while winter caters to skiing, snowboarding, and other snow-related activities.

Consider your preferences and desired experiences to choose the best time that matches with your travel plans, enabling you to immerse yourself completely in the charm and offerings of Oslo and Bergen.

Entry Requirements and Visa Information

Schengen Area: Norway is part of the Schengen Area, enabling individuals from specific countries to enter without a visa for short periods of up to 90 days within a 180-day period. Travellers from Schengen visa-exempt nations must verify their passport is valid for at least three months beyond their anticipated departure date.

Visa Requirements: Citizens of non-Schengen countries may require a Schengen visa to enter Norway. The visa application procedure normally requires supplying a valid passport, completed application form, trip itinerary, evidence of lodging, travel insurance, financial means, and extra papers depending on the purpose of the visit.

Visa Application Process

1. Application Submission: Visa applications are normally made at Norwegian embassies or consulates in the applicant's home country or the place of lawful residency. Online appointments could be required for submission.

2. Processing Time: Processing dates vary but normally take a few weeks. It's important to apply well in advance of your anticipated travel dates.

3. Additional Information: Applicants can be requested to give biometric data (fingerprints and a picture) throughout the application process.

Official Resources

- Embassy/Consulate Websites: Refer to the official websites of Norwegian embassies or consulates in your home country for accurate and up-to-date information on visa requirements, application procedures, and essential papers.

- Schengen Visa Information: Access the official Schengen visa website for basic guidelines and extensive information regarding visa requirements for travel inside the Schengen Areas.

Note for Travelers

- Transit Through Norway: Even if Norway is not your final destination, if you have a stopover or transit via a Norwegian airport, check whether you need a transit visa.

- Verify Requirements Early: Ensure you verify the visa requirements and start the application procedure early in advance of your intended trip to prevent any last-minute issues or delays.

- Travel Insurance: It's important to obtain travel insurance that covers medical bills, emergency evacuation, and other unforeseen occurrences during your stay in Norway.

Always consult official government sources or the Norwegian embassy/consulate in your country for the most current and updated visa information and procedures to guarantee a smooth entry into Norway.

Transportation Options

Navigating through Oslo and Bergen is made convenient with a variety of transportation modes, offering accessibility to explore these Norwegian cities and their surroundings. Here are the primary transportation options available:

Public Transportation

Oslo:

- Metro (T-bane) and Trams: Oslo's efficient metro system covers the city centre and surrounding areas, providing quick access to major attractions.

- Bus Services: Extensive bus routes complement the metro system, offering connectivity to various neighbourhoods and suburbs.

Bergen:

- Bybanen (Light Rail): Bergen's light rail system connects the city centre with the airport and neighbouring districts.

- Bus Network: Bergen boasts an extensive bus network, facilitating travel within the city and nearby regions.

Taxis and Ridesharing

Taxis are readily available in both Oslo and Bergen, but they tend to be more expensive. Ridesharing services also operate in these cities, providing an alternative mode of transportation.

Car Rentals

For travellers seeking flexibility and convenience, car rentals are available at airports and city centres. However, parking in city centres might be limited and expensive.

Cycling

Both Oslo and Bergen offer bike-friendly environments with dedicated bike lanes and rental services. Exploring the cities on a bicycle provides a unique and eco-friendly way to experience their charm.

Ferries

- Oslo: Ferries and boat tours operate from Oslo's harbour, offering scenic trips along the Oslo Fjord, providing views of the city's coastline and nearby islands.

- Bergen: Boat excursions and ferries depart from Bergen's harbour, offering tours of the fjords and nearby coastal areas.

Useful Tips:

- Citi Cards: Consider purchasing city travel cards or passes that offer unlimited travel on public transportation and discounts on attractions.

- Timetables and Apps: Access transportation timetables and plan routes using official transportation websites or mobile apps for real-time information and ease of navigation.

- Advance Planning: Plan your travel routes in advance, especially when using public transportation or booking specific tours or excursions, to optimise your itinerary.

By utilising these diverse transportation options, you can seamlessly traverse Oslo and Bergen, ensuring convenient access to their attractions, neighbourhoods, and surrounding natural beauty. Each mode of transport offers its own unique perspective on these enchanting Norwegian cities.

CHAPTER 2

EXPLORING OSLO

Oslo: The Capital of Norway

Cultural Hub: Oslo, Norway's capital, is a dynamic city packed with cultural attractions, historical sites, and a lively environment. Its combination of modern design among historic structures illustrates its rich past.

Green Spaces: Renowned for its plentiful green spaces, Oslo features parks like Vigeland Park, holding a wide collection of sculptures, and the expansive Frogner Park, excellent for leisurely strolls.

Waterfront Charm: Situated on the Oslo Fjord, the city's waterfront offers a magnificent location for activities such as boat cruises, kayaking, or simply enjoying the scenic views along the port.

Cultural Gems: Home to world-class institutions including the Viking Ship

Museum, the Munch Museum, and the Oslo Opera House, the city celebrates its cultural legacy via art, history, and music.

Culinary Delights: Oslo's culinary culture boasts a blend of traditional Norwegian cuisine with cosmopolitan cuisines, with various restaurants, cafés, and food markets offering varied gourmet experiences.

Bergen: The Coastal Gem

Historic Wharf District: Bergen's landmark Bryggen, a UNESCO World legacy Site, includes colourful Hanseatic structures going back to the 14th century, displaying the city's historical nautical legacy.

Gateway to Fjords: Positioned amid Norway's magnificent fjords, Bergen provides a great starting place for fjord excursions, cruises, and experiences exploring the breathtaking natural surroundings.

Scenic Surroundings: Surrounded by seven mountains, Bergen provides panoramic vistas and hiking options, including the famed Fløyen and Ulriken, accessible by a funicular and cable car, respectively.

Cultural Festivities: The city offers several cultural events and festivals throughout the year, from the Bergen International Festival to the vibrant Fish Market, giving an insight into local customs and talent.

Art and Music: Bergen shows its artistic flare through galleries, street art, and a dynamic music scene, developing talents and maintaining the region's creative past.

Two city overviews provide a look into the complex allure of Oslo and Bergen, allowing guests to immerse themselves in a tapestry of history, culture, natural beauty, and modern energy found inside two amazing Norwegian locations.

Oslos Top Attractions

Oslo, Norway's capital, brims with a wealth of attractions that appeal to varied interests, from history and art to nature and urban adventure. Here are some must-visit sites in Oslo:

1. Vigeland Sculpture Park (Frogner Park): This landmark park celebrates the life's work of artist Gustav Vigeland, showcasing over 200 magnificent sculptures created from bronze, granite, and wrought iron.

2. The Viking Ship Museum: Housing exceptionally well-preserved Viking ships, relics, and grave finds, this museum gives insights into Norway's naval history throughout the Viking Age.

3. The Oslo Opera House: Architecturally magnificent, the Opera House stands as a contemporary monument. Visitors may stroll on its sloping marble top, affording panoramic views of the city and fjord.

4. The Fram Museum: Dive into polar exploration history at the Fram Museum, holding the world's strongest polar ship, Fram, and reliving stories of trips to the Arctic and Antarctic.

5. Holmenkollen Ski Museum and Tower: Explore Norway's skiing past at the museum and enjoy stunning views from the top of the Holmenkollen Ski Jump Tower, a historic monument.

6. The Munch Museum: Dedicated to the works of famous artist Edvard Munch, this museum showcases an enormous collection of his paintings, including the classic 'The Scream.'

7. The National Gallery: Home to Norway's greatest public collection of paintings, the National Gallery shows a varied spectrum of Norwegian and foreign art, including pieces by Munch and other renowned painters.

8. Akershus Fortress: Delve into Oslo's history at this mediaeval stronghold, affording panoramic views of the city and holding numerous exhibitions, museums, and events.

Visiting these top sites gives a thorough grasp of Oslo's cultural history, artistic legacy, and historical importance, making your exploration of the city an enriching and unforgettable experience.

Neighborhood Guides

The throbbing heart of Oslo, the City Center, is a lively neighbourhood packed with historic structures, retail avenues, and cultural organisations.

Karl Johans gate: Oslo's main street, Karl Johans gate, spans from the Royal Palace to Oslo Central Station, surrounded with stores, restaurants, and noteworthy buildings including the Parliament and National Theatre.

Frogner & Vigeland Park

Overview: Frogner is a lovely suburb famed for its serene environment and the magnificent Vigeland Park, exhibiting remarkable sculptures by Gustav Vigeland.

Vigeland Park: This enormous park within Frogner showcases Gustav Vigeland's life's work, comprising over 200 sculptures, including the famed 'Monolith' and 'The Angry Boy.'

Grünerløkka & Mathallen

Overview: Grünerløkka, a dynamic and stylish district, emits a bohemian vibe with its chic cafés, vintage stores, and street art.

Mathallen: An epicurean paradise, Mathallen is Oslo's food hall, featuring a varied choice of gourmet dishes, beverages, and local vegetables from numerous exhibitors.

Bygdøy Peninsula

Overview: Bygdøy Peninsula is a refuge for museums, natural beauty, and historical attractions, accessible by ferry or bus from the city centre.

Museums: Bygdøy features many museums, including the Viking Ship Museum, the Fram Museum, the Kon-Tiki Museum, and the Norwegian nautical Museum, giving insights into nautical history and exploration.

Beaches and Nature: Bygdøy's coastline provides gorgeous walking routes, magnificent beaches like Huk Beach, and lush green spaces great for picnics or leisurely strolls.

Exploring these numerous areas of Oslo uncovers unique parts of the city's culture, history, and modern lifestyle, giving a well-rounded experience for tourists seeking various flavours of the Norwegian capital.

Cultural Experiences in Oslo and Bergen

Oslo

1. Norwegian National Opera & Ballet: Experience world-class performances in an architectural masterpiece. Attend opera, ballet, or concerts while enjoying stunning views of the Oslo Fjord.

2. Oslo's Music Scene: Explore Oslo's vibrant music scene with concerts ranging from classical to contemporary held in various venues, including Rockefeller Music Hall and Sentrum Scene.

3. Holmenkollen Ski Museum and Jump Tower: Immerse yourself in Norwegian skiing history at the museum and catch panoramic views from the iconic ski jump tower.

4. Oslo's Culinary Culture: Visit local markets like Mathallen and taste traditional Norwegian cuisine, including seafood delicacies like lutefisk and gravlax.

5. Historical Landmarks: Discover the city's history at Akershus Fortress and the Viking

Ship Museum, delving into Norway's mediaeval and Viking heritage.

Bergen

1. Bryggen's Hanseatic Heritage: Explore the historic Bryggen wharf, a UNESCO World Heritage Site, housing colourful wooden buildings and craft shops.

2. Festivals and Cultural Events: Participate in Bergen's vibrant cultural festivals, including the Bergen International Festival and Bergen Food Festival, showcasing art, music, and culinary delights.

3. Bergen's Art Scene: Admire local and international art at institutions like KODE Art Museums, hosting exhibitions featuring Norwegian and European art.

4. Fjord Cruises and Nature Walks: Embark on fjord cruises from Bergen, exploring Norway's stunning landscapes and picturesque fjords, a hallmark of the country's natural beauty.

5. Hanseatic Museum and Schøtstuene: Delve into Bergen's Hanseatic history at the Hanseatic Museum and Schøtstuene,

providing insights into the city's maritime past.

Engaging in these cultural experiences allows visitors to delve deeper into the history, arts, traditions, and natural wonders that Oslo and Bergen proudly offer, enriching their journey through Norway's cultural tapestry.

Exploring Oslo: Outdoor Adventures

1. Vigorous Hiking in Nordmarka: Escape into nature in Nordmarka, Oslo's huge wooded region with several hiking routes appropriate for all abilities. Experience tranquil lakes, lush forests, and magnificent vistas.

2. Cycling Along Akerselva River: Rent a bike and peddle down Akerselva, a lovely river running across the city. Explore historic landmarks, parks, and attractive

neighbourhoods while enjoying the quiet ambiance.

3. Oslo's Waterfront Activities: Engage in different water-based activities in the Oslo Fjord, such as kayaking, sailing, or boat trips. Relax on the beach in Huk, famous for sunbathing and swimming during warmer months.

4. Skiing and Winter Sports: During winter, appreciate Oslo's skiing culture by visiting neighbouring resorts like Holmenkollen Ski

Jump or Oslo Winter Park for skiing, snowboarding, or tobogganing.

5. Island Exploration: Take a boat to adjacent islands like Hovedøya or Langøyene for picnics, sunbathing, and leisurely hikes, affording a tranquil getaway from the city bustle.

6. Frognerparken Activities: Besides the statues in Vigeland Park, Frognerparken provides open places for picnics, running, or lounging amidst beautifully maintained gardens.

7. Camping in Oslomarka: For a unique experience, explore camping at Oslomarka, offering campsites, cabins, and an opportunity to interact with nature within a short distance from the city.

Exploring Oslo's outdoor attractions delivers a combination of natural beauty, recreational activities, and calm landscapes, appealing to outdoor lovers seeking adventure and tranquillity within the city's bounds.

Dining and Nightlife in Oslo

Dining Experiences

1. Culinary Diversity: Oslo features a diversified culinary scene, featuring traditional Norwegian food with cosmopolitan influences. Explore places like Maaemo (three Michelin stars) for a great dining experience or Mathallen Food Hall for a range of cuisines.

2. Seafood Delights: Indulge in Norway's famed seafood at places like Fiskeriet Youngstorget or Solsiden Restaurant,

tasting fresh fish, shrimp, and local delicacies.

3. Café Culture: Embrace Oslo's café culture by visiting prominent locations like Tim Wendelboe for outstanding coffee or Baker Hansen for pastries and Scandinavian delights.

4. Street Food Markets: For a casual eating experience, visit street food markets like Vulkan Street Food or Grønland Basar, providing varied delicacies from around the world.

Nightlife Options

1. A Vibrant Bar Scene: Explore Oslo's numerous bars, from sophisticated cocktail lounges like Himkok to ancient pubs like Schouskjelleren Mikrobryggeri, selling artisan brews.

2. Live Music Venues: Experience live music in places such as Blå, hosting numerous genres from jazz to electronic music, or Oslo's famed Rockefeller Music Hall for concerts and events.

3. Clubbing and Dancing: Enjoy Oslo's nightlife by dancing the night away at clubs like Jaeger or The Villa, noted for their energetic atmospheres and unique music selections.

4. Fjord Cruises and Night Tours: Opt for a fresh experience by going on nighttime fjord cruises or guided night excursions, affording spectacular views of the city lights from the sea.

Practical Tips

- Reservations: Make reservations, especially for prominent restaurants or sought-after nightlife locations, to assure a seat or access.

- Opening Hours: Note that certain restaurants and pubs could have different opening hours, with weekends often busier than weekdays.

- Journey: Plan your journey back to lodgings in advance, including public transport timetables or other options like taxis or ridesharing services.

Oslo's food scene and nightlife offer a rich tapestry of experiences, catering to varied interests and inclinations, making nights in the city as dynamic and pleasant as its daytime escapades.

CHAPTER 3

DISCOVERING BERGEN

Introduction to Bergen

Nestled along Norway's western coast, Bergen stands as a picturesque city adorned with a blend of natural beauty, historical charm, and cultural richness. As the gateway to the fjords and surrounded by seven stunning mountains, Bergen captivates visitors with its captivating landscapes and maritime heritage.

Historic Wharf District - Bryggen

At the heart of Bergen lies Bryggen, a UNESCO World Heritage Site characterised by its iconic Hanseatic buildings. These colourful wooden structures, dating back to the Hanseatic League in the 14th century, evoke tales of the city's seafaring past and trading prowess.

Fjords, Mountains, and Coastal Beauty

Surrounded by fjords, Bergen offers breathtaking vistas and opportunities for exploration. From the UNESCO-listed

Nærøyfjord and Hardangerfjord to the panoramic views atop Mount Fløyen and Mount Ulriken, Bergen's natural allure is unparalleled.

Cultural Vibrancy and Festivals

Bergen pulsates with cultural vitality, hosting various festivals and events throughout the year. The Bergen International Festival, Bergen Food Festival, and the Bergen International Film Festival showcase the city's artistic flair and culinary delights.

Artistic Heritage and Museums

Bergen nurtures its artistic legacy through institutions like the KODE Art Museums, displaying local and international art across multiple venues. The Hanseatic Museum and Schøtstuene provide glimpses into Bergen's maritime history and the Hanseatic period.

Outdoor Adventures and Exploration

Beyond its cultural offerings, Bergen invites visitors to partake in outdoor adventures, such as hiking the city's surrounding mountains, cruising through fjords, or experiencing the tranquillity of the nearby islands.

As a city steeped in history, blessed with natural wonders, and alive with cultural vibrancy, Bergen entices travellers to immerse themselves in its charm, promising an unforgettable journey through the heart of Norway's coastal splendour.

Discovering Bergen: Must-See Sights

1. Bryggen Hanseatic Wharf: Explore Bryggen's unique Hanseatic buildings, a UNESCO World Heritage Site, showcasing bright timber structures that harken back to Bergen's nautical heritage.

2. Fløibanen Funicular and Mount Fløyen: Ascend Mount Fløyen by the Fløibanen funicular for panoramic views of Bergen. Enjoy hiking routes, vistas, and family-friendly activities at the top.

3. Bergenhus Fortress and Rosenkrantz Tower: Discover Bergen's mediaeval history at the Bergenhus Fortress. Explore Rosenkrantz Tower, part of the stronghold, giving insights into the city's past.

4. Edvard Grieg's Troldhaugen: Visit the old residence of famed composer Edvard Grieg. Explore Troldhaugen's picturesque surroundings and watch performances commemorating Grieg's artistic legacy.

5. KODE Art Museums: Immerse yourself in art at the KODE Art Museums, featuring numerous locations showing Norwegian and international art, including pieces by Edvard Munch and Nikolai Astrup.

6. Fish Market (Fisketorget): Experience Bergen's unique fish culture at the Fish Market. Sample fresh seafood, fruits, and local delicacies while enjoying the lively market environment.

7. Bergen Aquarium (Akvariet i Bergen): Delve into aquatic life at the Bergen Aquarium. Witness a broad assortment of aquatic animals and participate in engaging exhibitions for all ages.

8. Hanseatic Museum and Schøtstuene: Gain insights into Bergen's Hanseatic past at the Hanseatic Museum and Schøtstuene, displaying the city's maritime tradition and commercial legacy.

9. Ulriken Cable Car: Take a cable car to the peak of Mount Ulriken, giving panoramic views of Bergen and options for hiking, eating, and outdoor excursions.

10. Naerøyfjord and Hardangerfjord Tours: Embark on breathtaking fjord cruises from Bergen to explore the UNESCO listed Nærøyfjord and the stunning Hardangerfjord, exploring Norway's dramatic landscapes.

These must-see places in Bergen offer a thrilling tour through the city's history, natural beauty, cultural richness, and maritime legacy, providing an enriching and unforgettable discovery of Norway's coastal treasure.

Exploring Bryggen

Bryggen, a famous seaside neighbourhood in Bergen, allows visitors to walk its cobblestone lanes surrounded with vibrantly coloured wooden structures. This UNESCO World Heritage Site stands as a tribute to Bergen's Hanseatic history and nautical legacy.

Immersing in History:

1. Hanseatic Museum and Schøtstuene: Explore these conserved merchant mansions turned museums, presenting insights into the Hanseatic League's commercial activity, lifestyle, and cultural impact in Bergen.

2. Walking Tour of Bryggen: Embark on a guided walking tour to dig into the district's history. Learn about the fires, restorations, and stories of the merchants who formerly prospered in these tight lanes.

Shopping and Artisanal Crafts:

3. Bryggen's Craft Shops: Browse among the boutiques and craft stores presenting traditional Norwegian handicrafts, jewellery, woollens, and souvenirs, allowing tourists to take home a piece of Bergen's culture.

Cultural Experiences:

4. Bryggens Museum: Visit the Bryggens Museum to explore archeological relics and displays depicting Bryggen's mediaeval past and the city's growth through time.

Dining with a View:

5. Waterside Cafés and Restaurants: Enjoy eating at waterfront restaurants serving fresh seafood specialties while taking up magnificent views of Vågen Harbor and the lively activity along the docks.

Practical Tips:

- Photography: Capture the brilliantly painted wooden structures and lovely lanes that highlight Bryggen's distinctive architectural attractiveness.

- Guided Tours: Consider taking guided tours or talks to obtain a greater knowledge of Bryggen's historical significance and cultural heritage.

Exploring Bryggen is a pleasant voyage through time, allowing visitors to uncover the layers of Bergen's maritime heritage, enjoy its cultural life, and admire the architectural grandeur of this ancient port region.

Fjord Tours and Cruises

Exploring the fjords around Bergen gives an unrivalled opportunity to observe Norway's spectacular natural landscapes and enchanting beauty. Here's how you may go on fjord excursions and cruises from Bergen:

1. Naerøyfjord and Hardangerfjord Tours: Join guided excursions or day trips from Bergen to the UNESCO-listed Nærøyfjord and the spectacular Hardangerfjord.

Activities: - Scenic Cruises: Experience stunning fjord tours, marvelling at towering cliffs, gushing waterfalls, and charming settlements dotting the fjord's coastlines.

- Village Visits: Stop in small settlements like Flåm, Gudvangen, or Ulvik along the Nærøyfjord and Hardangerfjord, embracing local culture and gorgeous surroundings.

2. Fjord Sightseeing Cruises: Various operators provide sightseeing excursions and cruises departing from Bergen, offering a look into the region's natural beauties.

Duration and Routes: - Half-Day Cruises: Shorter trips give brief glimpses of the fjords, excellent for people with limited time.

- Full-Day Tours: Longer tours allow for more complete exploration, sometimes including stops at significant fjord sites and picturesque overlooks.

3. Customised Private Tours: Opt for customised fjord trips suited to your interests, delivering a personalised and intimate experience of the fjords.

Customization Options: Boat Rentals: Charter a boat or hire a private guide for a customised route, giving flexibility and unique encounters.

- Specialised Activities: Arrange activities like kayaking, fishing, or trekking along the fjord's pathways for a unique trip.

Practical Tips:

- Weather Considerations: Check weather predictions and seasonal fluctuations while booking fjord trips to guarantee the greatest experience.

- Booking in Advance: Reserve excursions or cruises in advance, especially during high seasons, to guarantee preferred timings and prevent last-minute disappointments.

Exploring the beautiful Norwegian fjords from Bergen is a memorable adventure, allowing guests to immerse themselves in nature's majesty and observe the incomparable splendour of Norway's famous landscapes.

Hiking Trails and Nature Escapes

Exploring Bergen's surrounding countryside uncovers a treasure trove of hiking paths and tranquil getaways, allowing opportunity to immerse oneself in Norway's magnificent landscapes:

1. **Mount Fløyen:** Accessible by the Fløibanen funicular, Mount Fløyen provides picturesque routes ideal for all fitness levels, affording panoramic views of Bergen and its neighbouring fjords.

Activities: - Hiking Trails: Choose from various well-marked trails, such as the Fløysvingene or Brushytten walks, leading to vistas and ideal picnic sites.

- Outdoor Recreation: Engage in sports like mountain biking, zip-lining, or simply savour the serene ambiance amid nature.

2. Mount Ulriken: Ascend Mount Ulriken by the cable car for a selection of hiking paths, fascinating landscapes, and exhilarating excursions.

Activities: - Hiking Expeditions: Trails like the Vidden walk, linking Mount Ulriken to Mount Fløyen, provide hard yet rewarding experiences via different environments.

- Paragliding: For the daring, engage in paragliding trips from Mount Ulriken, affording spectacular airborne views of Bergen and its surrounds.

3. Vidden Trail: The Vidden Trail extends between Mount Ulriken and Mount Fløyen, giving an immersive hiking experience across stunning plateaus and rocky terrain.

Highlights: - Challenging Trek: This full-day climb requires energy but rewards hikers with beautiful panoramas of fjords, lakes, and the metropolis.

- Guided Tours: Join guided excursions or employ local guides for an improved understanding of the area's vegetation, animals, and geological aspects.

4. Fjord and Coastal Walks: Explore gorgeous coastline routes and fjord-side trails, giving tranquil getaways from metropolitan life.

Options: - Stoltzekleiven: This steep climb in Sandviksfjellet rewards hikers with beautiful views and a difficult exercise.

- Island Hopping: Ferry to adjacent islands like Askøy or Lysøen for calm strolls, enjoying serene surroundings away from the city's bustling.

Practical Tips:

- Prepare Adequately: Wear suitable footwear, pack water, food, and check weather conditions before beginning on hikes.

- Respect Nature: Follow established pathways, heed to signs, and maintain cleanliness to protect the natural beauty of these locations.

Bergen's hiking paths and nature getaways serve both ardent adventurers and casual explorers, guaranteeing stunning vistas, exciting walks, and an intimate touch with

Norway's beautiful landscapes.

CHAPTER 4

ACCOMMODATION OPTIONS IN OSLO AND BERGEN

Oslo:

1. Hotels: Oslo provides a selection of hotels catering to varied budgets and interests, from luxury lodgings like The Thief or Grand Hotel to mid-range options like Scandic or Comfort Hotel.

2. Hostels: Budget tourists might pick for hostels such as Anker Hostel or Oslo Hostel Haraldsheim, giving economical lodgings with shared amenities and sociable atmospheres.

3. Apartments and Rentals: Consider renting apartments or holiday rentals through companies like Airbnb or Booking.com for more spacious and homely lodgings, suited for families or extended vacations.

4. Boutique Hotels: Experience distinctive stays at boutique hotels like Hotel Continental or Amerikalinjen, offering individual services and different atmospheres.

Bergen:

1. Bryggen Hotels: Experience the beauty of Bergen's historic neighbourhood by staying in hotels inside Bryggen, such as Thon Hotel Bergen Brygge or Bergen Børs Hotel.

2. City Center Hotels: Explore lodgings in Bergen's city centre, featuring options like

Radisson Blu Royal Hotel Bergen or Zander K Hotel, offering convenience and closeness to activities.

3. Guesthouses and B&Bs: Discover charming guest houses or bed and breakfasts near Bergen, such as Ole Bull Hotel & Apartments or Villa Terminus, giving a more private and customised experience.

4. Fjord-side Retreats: Opt for lodgings near the fjords, such Solstrand Hotel & Bad or

Hotel Ullensvang, giving stunning views and access to wildlife.

Practical Tips:

- Booking in Advance: Especially during busy tourist seasons, it's important to reserve rooms well in advance to obtain preferred alternatives and pricing.

- Location Considerations: Choose lodgings based on closeness to attractions, public transit, or personal preferences, assuring convenience throughout your visit.

- Amenities and Reviews: Read reviews and examine services given by motels, such as Wi-Fi, breakfast, parking, or other particular requirements you might have.

Both Oslo and Bergen provide a broad choice of hotel alternatives catering to various interests, offering a comfortable and pleasurable stay for tourists experiencing these dynamic Norwegian towns.

Recommended Restaurants

Oslo:

1. Maaemo

- Cuisine: Innovative Nordic Cuisine - Overview: A three Michelin-starred restaurant delivering an extraordinary dining experience centred on locally sourced foods and inventive culinary presentations.

2. Fru K

- Cuisine: Modern Scandinavian - Overview: Known for its seasonal cuisine and devotion to Norwegian tastes, Fru K delivers a small yet classy eating ambiance.

3. Lofoten Fiskerestaurant

- Cuisine: Seafood - Overview: A seafood-centric restaurant serving fresh catches cooked in traditional Norwegian and modern techniques, overlooking Aker Brygge.

4. Smalhans

- Cuisine: Contemporary Norwegian - Overview: A relaxing cafe featuring a daily changing menu, focused on simple yet excellent meals using local food.

5. Brasserie Ouest

- Cuisine: French-inspired - Overview: Offering French-inspired food with a Norwegian twist, Brasserie Ouest features a sophisticated setting and an extensive wine selection.

Bergen:

1. Lysverket

- Cuisine: Nordic - Overview: Renowned for its inventive and seasonal menus, Lysverket provides Nordic meals prepared from locally sourced ingredients in a sophisticated atmosphere.

2. Colonialen

- Cuisine: Modern European - Overview: Comprising a mix of restaurants, cafés, and bakeries, Colonialen focuses on high-quality ingredients and elegant European cuisine.

3. Bare Vestland

- Cuisine: Norwegian - Overview: Aiming to emphasise the finest of West Norwegian products, Bare Vestland offers a modern perspective on traditional Norwegian meals.

4. Enhjørningen

- Cuisine: Seafood - Overview: Situated on the seaside, Enhjørningen specialises in seafood dishes, allowing customers to relish fresh catches while enjoying spectacular views.

5. Litteraturhuset

- Cuisine: Global - Overview: Combining a restaurant, cafe, and cultural centre, Litteraturhuset delivers a broad menu reflecting worldwide influences and local ingredients.

Practical Tips:

- Reservations: Consider making reservations, especially at fine dining places, to assure a table, especially during weekends or high seasons.

- Local Specialties: Explore meals that showcase local Norwegian delicacies or seasonal ingredients for a genuine culinary experience in both cities.

Shopping Guide

Oslo:

1. Karl Johans Gate

- Overview: Oslo's main shopping street, hosting a mix of international brands, department stores like Steen & Strøm, and local boutiques.

2. Aker Brygge

- Overview: A vibrant waterfront area offering a blend of high-end shops, design stores, and specialty shops, along with waterfront dining options.

3. Mathallen Oslo

- Overview: A food hall presenting a diverse range of Norwegian and international foods, perfect for buying local produce, spices, and culinary gifts.

4. Bogstadveien

- Overview: Known for its fashion outlets, independent stores, and trendy boutiques, Bogstadveien is a prime spot for clothing, accessories, and homeware.

5. Grunerløkka

- Overview: Explore this hip neighbourhood for vintage shops, art galleries, and eclectic stores, offering unique clothing, art, and alternative fashion.

Bergen:

1. Bryggen Shops

- Overview: Within the historic district, Bryggen houses unique souvenir shops, craft stores, and art galleries, offering traditional Norwegian gifts and local crafts.

2. Galleriet Shopping Center

- Overview: A modern shopping centre in the city centre with various shops, fashion outlets, and specialty stores catering to diverse shopping needs.

3. Strandgaten and Torgallmenningen

- Overview: Wander along these streets for a mix of fashion outlets, department stores, and local shops, providing a wide range of shopping options.

4. Fisketorget (Fish Market)

- Overview: Apart from fresh seafood, Fisketorget offers stalls with local crafts, souvenirs, and traditional Norwegian items perfect for gifting.

5. Xhibition Shopping Center

- Overview: An indoor shopping centre housing international brands, local boutiques, and accessory shops, ideal for diverse shopping preferences.

Practical Tips:

- Tax-Free Shopping: Visitors eligible for tax refunds can inquire about tax-free shopping options at participating stores and collect tax-free forms for reimbursement.

- Local Crafts and Souvenirs: Look for traditional Norwegian items like knitwear, woodwork, glassware, and silver jewellery for authentic souvenirs and gifts.

Health and Safety Tips

General Tips:

1. Travel Insurance: - Obtain comprehensive travel insurance covering medical emergencies, trip cancellations, and unforeseen catastrophes during your stay.

2. Emergency Contacts: - Save local emergency numbers, including police, ambulance, and necessary consulate or embassy contacts, in case of emergencies.

Oslo and Bergen:

1. Weather Preparedness: - Be ready for different weather conditions; carry proper clothing and gear for rain, wind, or cooler temperatures, especially during the winter months.

2. Safe Transportation: Utilise reputable and licensed transportation choices. Be cautious while crossing roads and utilise marked pedestrian crossings.

3. Safe Socialising: Be aware of your things in busy settings and public transit. Avoid leaving personal goods unattended.

Health Precautions:

1. Stay Hydrated and Rested: Maintain hydration, especially during vigorous activity or lengthy walks, and provide ample rest to avoid weariness.

2. Healthcare institutions: Familiarise yourself with area medical institutions and pharmacies, especially if you have specific health issues or require medication.

3. Food and Water Safety: Consume safe and sanitary food. Opt for bottled or purified water and avoid ingesting undercooked or unhygienically prepared food.

Outdoor Activities:

1. Hiking Safety: Plan hiking expeditions with adequate gear, maps, and alert someone about your schedule. Stay on approved routes and be careful of changing weather conditions.

2. Fjord excursions: When partaking in fjord cruises or boat excursions, adhere to safety recommendations supplied by tour operators and use life jackets if needed.

3. Sun Protection: Apply sunscreen and wear hats or sunglasses to protect yourself from the sun, especially during outside activities.

By emphasising health and safety precautions, maintaining awareness of your surroundings, and following recommended rules, you may assure a safe and pleasurable tour of Oslo and Bergen.

Useful Phrases and Local Etiquette

Basic Phrases:

1. Hello:

 - Oslo: "Hei" (hay)

 - Bergen: "Hei" (hay)

2. Goodbye:

 - Oslo: "Ha det" (haha deg)

 - Bergen: "Ha det" (haha deh)

3. Thank You:

- Oslo: "Takk" (tahk)

- Bergen: "Takk" (tahk)

4. Please:

- Oslo: "Vær så snill" (vair så snill)

- Bergen: "Vær så snill" (vær så snill)

Local Etiquette:

1. Respect Personal Space: Norwegians value personal space. Maintain a respectful distance during conversations and interactions.

2. Punctuality: Being on time is important. Arrive promptly for appointments, meetings, or tours.

3. Tipping: Tipping is not mandatory but appreciated for exceptional service. It's common to round up bills in restaurants.

4. Quietness in Public Spaces: Norwegians appreciate a peaceful environment. Keep conversations subdued in public places like public transport or restaurants.

5. Environmental Consciousness: Norway emphasises environmental preservation. Dispose of trash responsibly and respect nature while exploring.

6. Shoes Off Indoors: Some households and certain accommodations may expect visitors to remove their shoes before entering.

7. Greetings: A firm handshake and direct eye contact are common in greetings, along with a smile and a polite nod.

Additional Tips:

English Proficiency:

- Most locals speak excellent English. However, learning a few Norwegian phrases can be appreciated and helpful.

- Queueing Etiquette:

- Respect queues and wait your turn in public places, such as transportation stops or ticket counters.

Dress Code:

- Norway tends to be casual in dress. However, for finer dining or cultural events, smart casual attire is suitable.

Embracing local customs and phrases while observing local etiquette ensures a smoother and more culturally enriching experience during your visit to Oslo and Bergen.

CHAPTER 5

ONE WEEK ITINERARY FOR ALL TRAVELLERS

Week-Long Itinerary Catering to Different Travel Styles

Day 1: Arrival in Oslo

- Adventure Enthusiast:

  - Morning: Check-in and head to Holmenkollen Ski Museum & Tower for panoramic views.

- Afternoon: Explore Vigeland Park for unique sculptures.

- Evening: Dine på Grünerløkka.

- Cultural Immersion:

  - Morning: Visit the Viking Ship Museum.

  - Afternoon: Discover the Munch Museum and take a city walking tour.

  - Evening: Enjoy Nordic cuisine at Aker Brygge.

- Family-Friendly:

  - Morning: Norwegian Museum of Cultural History and park picnic.

  - Afternoon: Fram Museum exploration.

  - Evening: Oslo Fjord boat tour.

- Solo Traveler:

  - Morning: Grünerløkka exploration for coffee and vintage shops.

  - Afternoon: Nobel Peace Center visit.

  - Evening: Embrace local nightlife or attend a meetup.

Day 2: Oslo Cultural Delights

- Adventure Enthusiast:

  - Morning: Holmenkollen Ski Jump visit.

  - Afternoon: Oslo Opera House and city stroll.

  - Evening: Try local cuisine in Grünerløkka.

- Cultural Immersion:

  - Morning: Explore Akershus Fortress and Oslo City Hall.

  - Afternoon: Experience the Norwegian Opera & Ballet.

- Evening: Aker Brygge Dinner.

- Family-Friendly:

  - Morning: Viking Ship Museum.

  - Afternoon: Munch Museum visit.

  - Evening: Family dinner in Grünerløkka.

- Solo Traveler:

  - Morning: Visit the Viking Ship Museum.

  - Afternoon: Take a self-guided city tour.

- Evening: Explore Oslo's nightlife scene.

Day 3: Historical Insights

- Adventure Enthusiast:

- Morning: Oslo City Hall and museum visit.

- Afternoon: Akershus Fortress exploration.

- Evening: Relax with an Oslo Fjord cruise.

- Cultural Immersion:

  • Morning: Norwegian Museum of Cultural History.

  • Afternoon: Guided city tour.

  • Evening: Enjoy dinner in Aker Brygge.

- Family-Friendly:

  • Morning: City Hall and Oslo City Museum.

  • Afternoon: Aker Brygge and Oslo Fjord cruise.

  • Evening: Dinner på Grünerløkka.

- Solo Traveler:

  - Morning: Guided city tour.

  - Afternoon: Explore Oslo's landmarks.

  - Evening: Enjoy a local food tour or cooking class.

Day 4: Travel to Bergen

- Adventure Enthusiast:

  - Morning: Travel to Bergen.

  - Afternoon: Check-in and explore Bryggen.

  - Evening: Try local cuisine.

- Cultural Immersion:

  - Morning: Travel to Bergen.

  - Afternoon: Check-in and visit the KODE Art Museums.

  - Evening: Cultural performance.

- Family-Friendly:

  - Morning: Travel to Bergen.

  - Afternoon: Check-in and visit Bergen Aquarium.

  - Evening: Family dinner.

- Solo Traveler:

  - Morning: Travel to Bergen.

  - Afternoon: Check-in and stroll through Bryggen.

  - Evening: Dinner in a local restaurant.

Day 5: Bergen's Highlights

- Adventure Enthusiast:

  - Morning: KODE Art Museums visit.

  - Afternoon: Bergenhus Fortress exploration.

  - Evening: Cultural performance or concert.

- Cultural Immersion:

  • Morning: KODE Art Museums.

  • Afternoon: Bergen Aquarium and Fish
  Market.

  • Evening: Attend a cultural
  performance.

- Family-Friendly:

  • Morning: KODE Art Museums.

  • Afternoon: Bergen Aquarium and Fish
  Market.

  • Evening: Family dinner.

- Solo Traveler:

  - Morning: KODE Art Museums.

  - Afternoon: Bergenhus Fortress.

  - Evening: Attend a local music venue.

Day 6: Nature and Exploration

- Adventure Enthusiast:

  - Morning: Hike Mount Fløyen.

  - Afternoon: Visit the Old Bergen Museum.

  - Evening: Traditional Norwegian dinner.

- Cultural Immersion:

- Morning: Old Bergen Museum.

- Afternoon: Fantoft Stave Church visit.

- Evening: Enjoy local cuisine.

- Family-Friendly:

- Morning: Family hike på Mount Fløyen.

- Afternoon: Old Bergen Museum and Fantoft Stave Church.

- Evening: Traditional Norwegian dinner.

- Solo Traveler:

  - Morning: Solo hike på Mount Fløyen.

  - Afternoon: Explore Bergen's hidden gems.

  - Evening: Experience Bergen's nightlife.

Day 7: Fjord Excursion and Departure

- Adventure Enthusiast:

  - Morning: Fjord cruise from Bergen.

  - Afternoon: Last-minute exploration.

  - Evening: Departure.

- Cultural Immersion:

  - Morning: Fjord cruise.

  - Afternoon: Last-minute shopping or leisure walk.

  - Evening: Departure.

- Family-Friendly:

  - Morning: Family fjord cruise.

  - Afternoon: Final souvenir shopping.

  - Evening: Departure.

- Solo Traveler:

  - Morning: Fjord cruise from Bergen.

  - Afternoon: Last-minute sightseeing.

- Evening: Departure.

Tailoring each day's itinerary to suit various travel preferences allows for a diverse and enriching experience, ensuring a memorable week-long exploration of Oslo and Bergen for all types of travellers. Adjust activities according to personal interests and enjoy a fulfilling journey through these vibrant Norwegian cities.

APPENDIX

Travel Guides and Websites:

1. Visit Oslo Official Website: [Visit Oslo](https://www.visitoslo.com/en/)
Offers comprehensive information on attractions, events, accommodations, and travel tips for exploring Oslo.

2. Visit Bergen Official Website: [Visit Bergen](https://en.visitbergen.com/)

Provides detailed insights into Bergen's attractions, tours, cultural events, accommodations, and local tips.

Mobile Apps:

1. VisitOSLO App: Provides maps, event schedules, transportation details, and guides for exploring Oslo, available for iOS and Android.

2. Visit Bergen App: Offers information on attractions, tours, restaurants, and events in Bergen, available for iOS and Android.

Local Tour Operators:

1. Oslo City Sightseeing Tours: Various operators offer guided tours, fjord cruises, and city sightseeing tours showcasing Oslo's highlights.

2. Bergen Excursions and Fjord Tours: Explore local tour operators offering fjord cruises, hiking expeditions, and cultural experiences around Bergen.

Social Media and Forums:

1. Travel Forums (e.g., TripAdvisor, Reddit): Platforms like TripAdvisor and Reddit have

active communities where travellers share experiences, ask questions, and offer recommendations about visiting Oslo and Bergen.

2. Instagram and Facebook: Follow official city pages, travel bloggers, and local influencers to discover hidden gems, events, and insider tips for both cities.

Local Visitor Centers:

1. Oslo Visitor Centre: Located centrally, offering brochures, maps, and guidance on city attractions, tours, and events.

2. Bergen Tourist Information Centre: Provides assistance, maps, and information about Bergen's attractions, activities, and local happenings.

Leverage these resources, both online and offline, to gather comprehensive information, local insights, and real-time updates, ensuring a fulfilling and informed exploration of Oslo and Bergen.

CONCLUSION

Embracing Oslo and Bergen

As your adventure through the dynamic cities of Oslo and Bergen draws to a conclusion, it's time to reflect on the fascinating experiences, breathtaking scenery, and cultural treasures you've experienced during your tour.

Oslo and Bergen, two separate yet equally enthralling cities, have welcomed you with open arms, delivering a combination of history, art, nature, and an insight into the heart of Norwegian culture. From the spectacular sculptures in Vigeland Park to the quaint UNESCO-listed Bryggen, each corner exposed a tale, a piece of history, and a new dimension of these remarkable sites.

In Oslo, you've immersed yourself in the creative cultural scene, dived into the rich Viking past, and embraced the contemporary Scandinavian lifestyle. The colourful energy of Grünerløkka, the architectural wonders of the Opera House, and the serene serenity of the Oslo Fjord all left lasting memories.

In Bergen, the beautiful fjords, colourful wooden buildings of Bryggen, and the busy fish markets have painted a stunning tapestry of this coastal treasure. Exploring its museums, art galleries, and relishing the seafood pleasures have afforded views into Bergen's rich maritime past and modern artistry.

The chapters of this travel book have attempted to arm you with insights, recommendations, and practical ideas to make your vacation a seamless and satisfying experience. From cultural lovers to adventure seekers, families to single travellers, each itinerary was developed to suit various interests and inclinations, delivering a bespoke vacation for everybody.

As you wave farewell to these wonderful cities, may the memories of the breathtaking vistas, kind hospitality, and the cuisines of Norway stay on. Let the soul of Oslo and Bergen linger with you, motivating future journeys and begging you to return and experience even more of Norway's beauties.

Remember, this travel guide barely touches the surface of the richness these places possess. The pleasure of adventure rests in the personal discoveries, the unexpected experiences, and the relationships established with the places you visit.

Oslo and Bergen anxiously await your return, ready to unravel new tales, create more experiences, and continue fueling your wanderlust. Until we meet again, may your travels be blessed with joy, discovery, and a sense of adventure.

Safe travels and may the appeal of Norway's beauty stay near to your heart.

Takk for besøket! (Thank you for the visit!)

Printed in Great Britain
by Amazon

39753394R00089